CELEBRATING
DRAGON BOAT FESTIVAL

Celebrating Dragon Boat Festival

EUGENIA CHU

Illustrated by Eliza Hsu Chen

Celebrating Dragon Boat Festival

All Rights Reserved
Copyright © 2024 Eugenia Chu
Miami, Florida

The opinions expressed in this manuscript are solely the opinions of the author. The author has represented and warranted full ownership and/or legal right to publish all the materials in this book.

All rights reserved. No part of this publication may be reproduced, distributed, or transmitted in any form or by any means, including photocopying, recording, or other electronic or mechanical methods, without the prior written permission of the publisher, except in the case of brief quotations embodied in critical reviews and certain other noncommercial uses permitted by copyright law.

Limitation of liability/disclaimer of warranty: the author makes no representations or warranties with respect to the accuracy or completeness of the contents of this work and specifically disclaim all warranties, including without limitation, warranties of fitness for a particular purpose. No warranty may be created or extended by sales or promotional materials. The fact that an individual, organization or website is referred to in this work as a citation in and/or potential source of further information does not mean that the author endorses the information, the individual, organization or website may provide or recommendations they/it may make. Further, reader should be aware that any websites listed in this work may have changed or disappeared between when this work was written when it is read.

Paperback ISBN: 978-1-7334808-9-5
Hardcover ISBN: 979-8-9902698-0-4

Library of Congress Control Number: 2024905851

Illustrated by: Eliza Hsu Chen

Edited by: Athena Cullens

http://eugeniachu.com

To my Brandon — again and again

CONTENTS

What is the Dragon Boat Festival?
1

History and Folklore
3

Preparation
7

How to Celebrate
10

Around the World
14

Culture Corner
19

Learn to Say It!
27

Glossary
28

Resources
31

WHAT IS THE DRAGON BOAT FESTIVAL?

T he Dragon Boat Festival, also known as the Double Fifth Festival, is a traditional Chinese holiday held on the fifth day of the fifth month of the Chinese **lunisolar calendar**. This is usually in late May or June on the **Gregorian calendar**, which is the most used calendar in the world.

The festivities vary from region to region, but most people celebrate by holding dragon boat races and eating sticky rice dumplings called ***zòngzi* (粽子)**. The Dragon Boat Festival is usually associated with the legend of Qu Yuan, a former king's advisor and poet.

The festival was long observed in communities as a cultural holiday, informally. In 2008, it was officially recognized as a public holiday in China. On October 30th, 2009, it was added to the **UNESCO Representative List of the Intangible Cultural Heritage of Humanity**. The list helps to safeguard and raise awareness of this holiday and its importance.

Similar holidays are celebrated in other East and Southeast Asian countries. In Mandarin Chinese, the Dragon Boat Festival is called *Duānwǔ Jié* (端午节).

Dragon boat racing is now an internationally recognized sport and is practiced in more than 50 countries, with competitions held around the world!

HISTORY AND FOLKLORE

Today, the Dragon Boat Festival, or *Duānwǔ Jié* (端午节), is considered a happy occasion that focuses on fun, health, and reunion. But the origins of this holiday are not so cheery.

THE LEGEND OF QU YUAN

There are many origin stories, but the most well-known is the legend of Qu Yuan.

Qu Yuan was a beloved patriotic poet and top advisor for the Kingdom of Chu during the **Warring States**

Period (475–221 BC). Qu Yuan dedicated his life to assisting the king in building a strong State of Chu. However, he was **exiled** when he opposed the king's plans to join the state of Qin.

When the state of Qin overthrew and took over the capital of Chu, Qu Yuan drowned himself in the Miluo River in protest on the fifth day of the fifth lunar month. The grieving villagers rushed out in boats to try to save him but failed. In an effort to save his body from being eaten by fish, they beat drums, thrashed the water with paddles, and threw rice dumplings in the river to distract the fish.

THE LEGEND OF WU ZIXU

Another competing myth from South China is that of Wu Zixu, who, like Qu Yuan, was also a loyal advisor whose advice was ignored by the king. However, according to this legend, the king forced Wu Zixu to take his own life and his body was dumped in the river on the fifth day of the fifth month. Afterwards, Wu Zixu was considered a river god.

Due to the many similarities in the two legends, many think they became mixed with one another over the centuries.

THE LEGEND OF CAO E

Another lesser-known legend about the Dragon Boat Festival is in memory of a young girl named Cao E. Cao E lived with her father in a small village. The details of the story vary, but the main idea is that her father fell into the river and never returned home. Cao E walked along the river day and night searching for her father. On the fifth day of the fifth month of the lunar year, she went into the river, too. Days later, villagers found the bodies of Cao E and her father together. Cao E is remembered for her love for her father, and the festival is dedicated to her sacrifice.

THE MONTH OF POISON

While the Legend of Qu Yuan is the most popular origin story, there is evidence that the Dragon Boat Festival, or *Duānwǔ Jié* (端午节), actually came before the death of Qu Yuan (as well as Wu Zixu and Cao E) and was originally regarded as a traditional medical and health festival.

Since ancient times, the fifth lunar month has been considered an unlucky month. It is known to some as the "month of poison" because the dreaded "five poisonous creatures" (五毒 *wǔdú*) begin to come out. Traditionally, the five creatures are centipedes, scorpions, snakes, toads, and spiders — oh my!

Additionally, during the early hot days of summer, people would become sick easily. This made the month seem evil, so people in ancient times regarded it as an important time to prevent diseases and keep evil spirits away. It is believed that this led to the tradition of wearing fragrant pouches or sachets containing flowering plants like **mugwort**, called ***xiāng bāo*** (香包), as well as hanging certain medicinal plants like **wormwood** and **calamus** on doors. Since the shape of calamus leaves is like that of a sword, and it produces a strong smell, it is believed that calamus can keep pests as well as evil spirits away. As a result, the Dragon Boat Festival is also called the "Calamus Festival" (***Chāngpú Jié*** 菖蒲节).

PREPARATION

During the Dragon Boat Festival, or *Duānwǔ Jié* (端午节), people often participate in or attend dragon boat races and other festivities. Before the big day, some people prepare by:

- making or purchasing sticky rice dumplings, called *zòngzi* (粽子);
- hanging mugwort and calamus on doors and windows;
- making or purchasing perfume pouches or *xiāng bāo* (香包); and
- braiding silk threads of five colors (green, red, white, black, and yellow) to give to children.

Now everyone is ready to celebrate!

VARIETIES OF ZÒNGZI (粽子)

There are mainly two tastes to *zòngzi* (粽子): sweet (generally preferred in northern China) or savory (generally preferred in southern China). Here are a few popular styles of *zòngzi* (粽子):

Cantonese-Style

Guangdong *zòngzi* (粽子) are usually large and have special shapes. They are either sweet with dates, walnuts, or bean paste, or savory with ham, egg, beef, or chicken.

Beijing-Style

Beijing *zòngzi* (粽子) are small and are in the shape of a triangle or rectangle. People often use jujube and sweet bean paste as fillings.

Shanghai-Style

There are two types of Shanghai-style *zòngzi* (粽子). One is savory while the other is sweet. A popular savory filling includes pork belly or chicken, shiitake mushrooms, and salted duck egg. The sweet style *zòngzi* (粽子) is often filled with red bean paste and is sometimes even dipped in sugar.

Taiwan-Style

The Taiwanese are accustomed to making their *zòngzi* (粽子) with different kinds of meat and seafood, and most of them have a salty and sweet taste.

HOW TO CELEBRATE

Dragon Boat Festival customs vary from region to region, but they usually share several features which can be roughly divided into two groups. One is to memorialize heroes, such as Qu Yuan, while the other aims to fend off evil and keep people healthy.

MEMORIALIZING HEROES

Eating and Gifting Zòngzi (粽子)

Zòngzi (粽子) is the most traditional Dragon Boat Festival food and is related to Qu Yuan's commemoration. It is an important part of the festival, just like turkey is at Thanksgiving. Families make (or purchase from restaurants and bakeries) sticky rice dumplings and pass them out as gifts, receive them, and eat them. They are usually wrapped in triangle or rectangle shapes within bamboo or reed leaves and tied with soaked stalks or colorful silky cords.

Participating In or Attending Dragon Boat Races

Dragon boat racing is the most important activity of the Dragon Boat Festival and also relates to the legend of Qu Yuan. Many places in China, as well as around the world, hold dragon boat races on long, narrow, wooden boats to celebrate the festival on the fifth day of the fifth lunar month.

The boats are often shaped and decorated to look like a Chinese dragon and usually hold 30-60 rowers. During the races, dragon boat teams paddle to the sound of beating drums. It is said that the winning team will have good luck and a happy life in the following year.

KEEPING PEOPLE HEALTHY AND FENDING OFF EVIL

Hanging Mugwort and Calamus

During the Dragon Boat Festival, people (mostly in rural areas) hang Chinese mugwort and calamus on their doors or walls. This is to deter flies, mosquitoes, and other insects, as well as to ward off disease and evil spirits. The purpose is to bring health and good luck to the family. This practice is not as common in the cities.

Wearing Scented Sachets

Parents often prepare scented sachets or pouches, called *xiāng bāo* (香包), for their children to protect them from evil. They sew colorful silk cloth into pouches or purses (or they buy them) which they fill with perfumes, mugwort, or herbal medicines. The children wear the *xiāng bāo* (香包) around their necks or tied to the front of their clothes during the Dragon Boat Festival.

Five Color String

Green, red, white, black, and yellow are lucky colors in ancient China. Another tradition to ward off evil, bad luck, or misfortune is for parents to give their children five threads of those colors during the Festival, often in the form of a five-color braided string bracelet. Some believe that if you throw them into the water after you wear them, you can wash away illness and disease.

Celebrating the Dragon Boat Festival plays a crucial role in preserving traditional Chinese customs and passing them on to future generations. It serves as a reminder of the country's rich cultural heritage and fosters a sense of national identity and pride. It is also a time for families to come together and strengthen their bonds by spending quality time together, creating cherished memories that last a lifetime.

AROUND THE WORLD

In addition to China, many other countries also celebrate the Dragon Boat Festival or a version of it. Some countries like Malaysia, Indonesia, and Singapore celebrate with dragon boat racing and *zòngzi* (粽子), similar to how they celebrate in China. However, the Dragon Boat Festival is not a public holiday in those countries. Here are a few examples of how a few other countries celebrate the Dragon Boat Festival.

TAIWAN

In addition to dragon boat races, hanging up mugwort, and making *zòngzi* (粽子) and scented sachets, the Taiwanese also celebrate the festival with egg balancing competitions. It is believed that if you can balance an egg on its end at noon, you will have good luck in the coming year!

SOUTH KOREA

In South Korea, Dano or Gangneung Danoje Festival, is another version of the Dragon Boat Festival. It is a month-long festival that begins by brewing sacred liquor to honor deities or gods. Various folk activities and events are held, such as making Dano (Duanwu) fans, swinging, performing traditional mask dances, and washing hair in calamus water.

VIETNAM

During the Dragon Boat Festival, Tết Đoan Ngọ, Vietnamese people prepare glutinous rice with a blend of spices to thank their ancestors and go to pagodas or temples to pray for good health and good fortune. Parents wipe a type of wine on their children to drive away insects. Children wear a lucky charm weaved out of colorful silk threads. In addition to the scented pouches, people may also hang red paper cutouts to ward off evil spirits and bring good luck.

JAPAN

The Japanese version of the Dragon Boat Festival is called Kodomo no hi (formerly Tango no sekku), also known as Children's Day. People believe iris, similar to calamus, can chase away sickness and evil spirits, so they hang them in and on their homes, sleep with them under their pillows, bathe in iris/calamus water, and drink iris/calamus wine. Boys also play games where they hit the ground with bundles of leaves or reeds. Whoever makes the loudest noise, without breaking the bundle, wins! The Japanese decorate their houses with samurai warrior figurines for protection and carp streamers for success.

THE UNITED STATES

On the day of the Dragon Boat Festival, many Chinese families in the USA will make or buy *zòngzi* (粽子). Dragon boat races have also become popular cultural events in the USA, and large cities like Los Angeles, San Francisco, Boston, New York, and Denver hold large-scale dragon boat races regularly.

THE UNITED KINGDOM

Dragon Boat Festival racing first featured competitively in the UK in 1980, and now the UK arguably holds the largest Dragon Boat Race in all of Europe! The Royal Family even gets in on the fun. The Prince of Wales started a Dragon Boat Race in London, the Queen Mother has launched a Dragon Boat, and Prince William has raced regularly.

CANADA

Dragon Boat Races are held almost every year in the main cities of Canada, including Vancouver, Toronto, and Montreal. Boat racing lovers from all over the world come to participate. The Concord Pacific Dragon Boat Festival is North America's largest Dragon Boat Festival and includes food, entertainment, fine arts, children's programming, and some of the world's most competitive dragon boat racing!

GERMANY

In 1989, dragon boat racing was imported to Germany, with the first Dragon Boat Festival to mark the 800th anniversary of the port of Hamburg. After 1991, the races moved to Frankfurt and have continued to this day.

> Some believe that if it rains on the festival day, there will be a poor harvest; whereas if it's sunny, there will be good fortune all year long!

CULTURE CORNER

Dragon Boat Festival is a special occasion where people participate in many fun activities. Try these at home with family and friends:

- *Zòngzi* (粽子) Recipe
- Stand an Egg Up
- Boiled Egg Contest
- Paper Boat Craft
- Lucky Five Color Braided String Bracelet

ZÒNGZI (粽子) RECIPE*

Dragon Boat Festival is all about *zòngzi* (粽子), so of course we had to include a simple recipe for you to try!

Makes: 15-20
Cook time: 1-3 hours
Prep time: 1-2 hours (plus marinating overnight)

What you'll need: 40-50 bamboo leaves, string

1 pound pork belly
2 pounds glutinous (sweet) rice
Fried shallots
3/4 cup soy sauce

Salt/pepper to taste
Optional: mushrooms, peanuts, mung beans, Chinese sausage, anything else you like

1. Cut the pork belly into small chunks, add soy sauce and salt/pepper, and let it sit overnight to marinate.

    Note: you can substitute pork with any meat and/or add any of the above options.

2. Wash the glutinous rice and soak in water.
3. Wash the bamboo leaves then boil them with a tablespoon of oil for a few minutes until soft.
4. Once cool, coil one or two bamboo leaves into the shape of a cone. Have the ends of the leaves meet up at the top. If a leaf rips, simply add another over it.
5. Fill a third of the cone with glutinous rice (about 1 tablespoon) and add 1-2 pieces of the pork belly and fried shallot (and/or any other filling) on top. Then, cover it with more sticky rice to about an inch below the rim of the cone (the more space you leave the easier it will be to fold).
6. Wrap it into a pyramid shape by folding down one side then the other, and finally folding the remaining length of the leaves down.
7. Bind the whole thing with string. Make sure rice cannot fall out of the cone.
8. Steam or boil the wrapped *zòngzi* (粽子) for at least one hour. Longer if you like the rice softer or if the *zòngzi* (粽子) is very large.

Note: You can do Steps 1-3 the day before. Once you get the hang of wrapping the zòngzi (粽子) (may take a few tries), it's fun! And the end product is so delicious!

*For a more detailed recipe with photos and videos, go to https://eugeniachu.com/zongzi-recipe/

STAND AN EGG UP

Believe it or not, you can balance an egg on its end on Dragon Boat Festival day. Try it at noon! The reason it works is most likely due to the fact that it's the **summer solstice**. At around noon on this day, the sun's pull on the Earth is at its strongest and eggs can stand on their end because of it.

Egg(s)

1. Boil 1 egg (or more).
2. At noon on the Dragon Boat Festival day, try to stand the egg up with the wider end on the bottom.
3. Some say if you succeed in making an egg stand up, you will have good luck for the year!

BOILED EGG CONTEST

The Boiled Egg Contest is so fun and super easy!

Boiled eggs
Prizes

1. Each player receives a boiled egg.
2. The players take turns pushing their eggs into one another's.
3. When an egg is cracked on two sides, that player is out.
4. The last player with one or zero cracks wins! Some say the winner will have good luck the rest of the year!

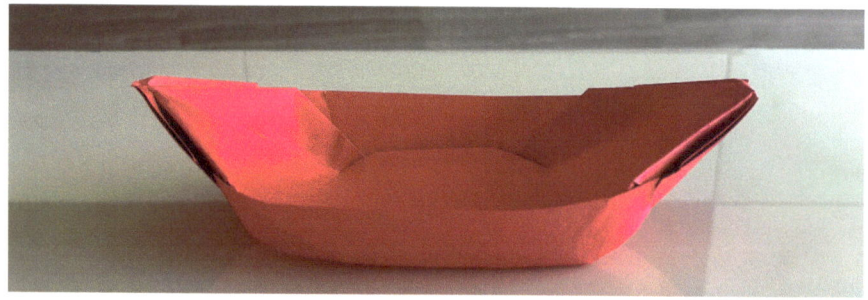

PAPER BOAT CRAFT*

Paper boats are fun to decorate and for racing!

Paper

Markers or stickers for decorating (optional)

Wax or tape to make paper water resistant (optional)

1. Fold a sheet of paper in half lengthwise.
2. Fold the paper from each side towards the crease.
3. On one side, fold the two ends up into a triangle.
4. Fold again to form a longer triangle.
5. Fold the bottom twice.
6. Repeat steps 3, 4, and 5 on the other side.
7. Turn it inside out and you have a paper boat!

Make the boat your own by decorating it however you like. If you want to make it water resistant so it can float, cover the bottom with wax or tape. Place them in the water and push or blow them. Use your imagination to come up with other ways to race your new paper boats. You can even add light toys to sit in the boat! So much fun!

*For a video tutorial, go to https://eugeniachu.com/paper-boat-craft/

LUCKY FIVE COLOR BRAIDED STRING BRACELET

Make your own string bracelet to ward off evil, bad luck, or misfortune!

Five different colors of string (or yarn or ribbon): green, red, white, black, and yellow

Scissors

Tape

Easy method:

1. Cut the strands of string about 20-25 inches long.
2. Tie the five strands of string together at one end — leave about two to three inches at the top so you can tie it on later.
3. Tape the tied end down to the table so it doesn't move.
4. Separate the strands into three groups (2-2-1).

5. Braid normally.
6. When you reach the end, tie the ends together to form a bracelet. Cut off any excess.

Difficult Method:

1. Do Steps 1 through 3 above.
2. Number the strands from 1 to 5, from right to left, to help keep track of the strands to start.
3. Place Strand 1 over Strand 2 and under Strand 3. Strand 1 is now between Strands 3 and 4.
4. Do the same on the other side: Place Strand 5 over Strand 4 and under Strand 1.
5. Place Strand 2 over Strand 3 and under Strand 5.
6. Place Strand 4 over Strand 1 and under Strand 2.
7. Continue this over-under pattern until you reach the end.
8. Tie the ends together to form a bracelet. Cut off any excess.

Now you have your own Lucky Five Color Braided String Bracelet to show off and to keep you safe and healthy. Make more to give to your friends and share the luck!

Note: if you want the bracelet to be thicker, double (or triple) up on each color string. Treat each color as one strand and follow the directions above. Have fun!

LEARN TO SAY IT!

One would think that saying "Happy Dragon Boat Festival" (端午快乐 *Duānwǔjié kuàilè*) would be an appropriate greeting, but it may not be because the holiday: 1) commemorates Qu Yuan (or other local heroes) and so this festival is to mourn his death; and 2) marks the month of poison and the avoidance of illness — not exactly a "happy" event!

Here are a few common and more appropriate phrases people say to each other during the Dragon Boat Festival:

Duānwǔjié ānkāng!
端午安康!
HAVE A SAFE AND HEALTHY DRAGON BOAT FESTIVAL!

Yuàn nǐguò yīgè nánwàng de duānwǔ jié!
愿你过一个难忘的端午节!
MAY YOU HAVE A MEMORABLE DRAGON BOAT FESTIVAL!

Zhōngxīn zhù nǐ duānwǔ jié xìngfú, ānkāng, měimǎn!
衷心祝你端午节幸福、安康、美满!
I SINCERELY WISH YOU HAPPINESS, HEALTH AND SUCCESS DURING THE DRAGON BOAT FESTIVAL!

GLOSSARY

Calamus: an aquatic plant also known as sweet flag

Chāngpú Jié (菖蒲节): Calamus Festival, another name for Dragon Boat Festival

Custom: a way of acting that is usual or accepted for a person or group

Duānwǔ Jié (端午节): Dragon Boat Festival in Mandarin Chinese

Dynasty: a family of rulers in a country

Emperor: a ruler who has total control of a country or region

Exile: being banned from one's country, usually for political reasons

Folklore: traditional customs, tales (myths and legends), sayings, dances, or art forms preserved among a people

Gregorian calendar: the calendar most countries use (the US has been using it since 1752!)

Lunar month: the time it takes the Moon to pass through all of the moon phases — about 29.5 days

Legend: a story with some basis in history and geography and tends to mention people or events

Lunisolar calendar: a calendar based on the phases of the moon (moon's orbit around the Earth), the movement of the sun (Earth's orbit around the sun), and the seasons

Mugwort: a plant of the daisy family with aromatic leaves that are dark green above and whitish below

Myth: a symbolic story that is passed down about how or why something came to be

Sacrifice: an act of offering something precious to a deity or god

Summer Solstice: the longest day of the year when the Earth's North Pole is tilted closest to the sun

UNESCO Representative List of the Intangible Cultural Heritage of Humanity: list to help protect and bring awareness of, important practices, knowledge, or skills that are part of a place's cultural heritage (a community's culture, values, and traditions)

Warring States Period: the three centuries when various rival Chinese states battled for land and dominance. Ultimately the Qin state won and established the first unified Chinese state

Wormwood: a woody shrub with a bitter taste, often used in medicine

Xiāng bāo (香包): scented sachets or pouches

Zòngzi (粽子): Chinese rice dish made of glutinous (sticky) rice stuffed with meat and/or other fillings and wrapped in bamboo or other flat leaves and cooked by steaming or boiling

> The dragon is included in the festival's decorations to bring good fortune and to ward off evil spirits because it symbolizes power, strength, and good luck.

RESOURCES

Educational websites with fun activities for kids:

- MissPandaChinese.com
- ChalkAcademy.com

Museums to visit:

- **New York City:** Museum of Chinese in America | mocanyc.org

- **Washington DC:** Chinese American Museum DC | chineseamericanmuseum.org

- **Los Angeles:** Chinese American Museum | camla.org

- **San Jose:** Chinese American Historical Museum | chcp.org

- **San Francisco:** Chinese Historical Society of America | chsa.org

- **Chicago:** Chinese American Museum of Chicago | ccamuseum.org

- **Portland:** Portland Chinatown Museum | portlandchinatownmuseum.org

- **Seattle:** Wing Luke Museum | wingluke.org

ABOUT THE AUTHOR

Eugenia Chu is an attorney turned stay-at-home mom turned multi-award winning and best selling author. She is Chinese-American and lives on a magical beach in Miami with her husband, Bob, son, Brandon, and dog, Dash.

Unable to find children's story books that included Chinese language or culture when Brandon was younger, she began writing them herself. Brandon is the inspiration for all her books.

Eugenia enjoys presenting her books at schools, libraries, museums, and festivals. She is an avid reader who delights in writing, traveling, yoga, and drinking too much coffee.

Eugenia is also the author of: *Brandon Makes Jiǎozi* (餃子); *Brandon Goes to Beijing – Běijīng* (北京); *Brandon Goes to Hong Kong – Xiānggǎng* (香港); *Celebrating Chinese New Year*; *Celebrating Mid-Autumn Festival;* and a contributing author to *Once Upon a Plate – A Culinary Journey Through Stories..*

Visit https://linktr.ee/eugeniachu to learn more about the author and her books, or to schedule an author visit.

ABOUT THE ILLUSTRATOR

Eliza Hsu Chen is an illustrator and graphic designer. Born to Taiwanese parents in Brazil, she was raised in Paraguay, and then moved to Miami when she was six. Her love for art grew during her years at Design and Architecture Senior High where she majored in architecture. She received the Posse scholarship and earned a bachelors in graphic design and marketing from Syracuse University. Visit ElizaHsuChen.com to see more of her work.

www.ingramcontent.com/pod-product-compliance
Lightning Source LLC
Chambersburg PA
CBHW042055060526
44119CB00115B/294